GRATEFUL

GRATEFULNESS IS *observation.*

IT'S PAYING CLOSE ATTENTION. IT'S NOTICING THE THINGS THAT ARE ALREADY HERE AND PAUSING LONG ENOUGH TO SEE THEM AND TO THINK, *LOOK AT THIS—ISN'T THIS GOOD?* GRATEFULNESS IS A WAY OF SHINING A LIGHT ON THINGS; IT'S A WAY OF SEEING DEEPLY, AND OF LETTING THAT SEEING RIPEN INTO APPRECIATION.

WHEN WE MOVE THROUGH THE WORLD WITH GRATEFULNESS, WHEN WE NOTICE THE GOOD THINGS, SUDDENLY THE GOOD THINGS ARE EVERYWHERE, AND THE DETAILS AND THE PEOPLE AND THE MOMENTS OF EACH DAY TRANSFORM. THEY GO FROM BEING THE THINGS WE EXPECT INTO BEING SOMETHING EXCEPTIONAL. GRATEFULNESS MAKES ABUNDANCE FROM THE EVERYDAY.

WHAT ARE YOU SHINING A LIGHT ON TODAY?
WHAT ARE YOU NOTICING HERE AND NOW?

What are you grateful for?

...FOR SMALL THINGS

AND EVERYDAY *joys.*

TAKE A TASTE... LIFE IS SO ENDLESSLY DELICIOUS.

Ruth Reichl

GRATEFUL FOR
THE SWEETNESS
OF EACH DAY.

WITH FREEDOM, BOOKS, FLOWERS AND THE MOON, WHO COULD NOT BE HAPPY?

Oscar Wilde

GRATEFUL FOR
THE ESSENTIALS
OF HAPPINESS.

...SEE THE MIRACULOUS IN THE COMMON.

Ralph Waldo Emerson

GRATEFUL FOR EXTRAORDINARY ORDINARY THINGS.

...THE LITTLE THINGS ARE INFINITELY
THE MOST IMPORTANT.

Sir Arthur Conan Doyle

WHAT SMALL THINGS
IN YOUR LIFE ADD UP
TO SOMETHING BIG?

...FOR *perfect* MOMENTS

AND *ordinary* DAYS.

...LOVE MOMENTS FOR THEMSELVES.

Gwendolyn Brooks

GRATEFUL FOR
EVERYTHING THERE
IS TO LOVE, HERE
AND NOW.

...LOOK AT YOUR LIFE AND SEE
HOW PERFECT IT IS.

Lev Grossman

GRATEFUL FOR THE
EASE AND ENJOYMENT
IN THIS DAY.

THAT'S THE THING WITH MAGIC.
YOU'VE GOT TO KNOW IT'S STILL
HERE, ALL AROUND US...

Charles de Lint

GRATEFUL FOR THE WONDER OF THIS TIME AND PLACE.

IT SHINES LIKE A LITTLE DIAMOND... THIS MOMENT.

Jean-Paul Sartre

WHAT SPARKLES
IN YOUR LIFE
RIGHT NOW?

...FOR FRIENDS, FAMILY,
AND *good* PEOPLE.

EACH FRIEND REPRESENTS A WORLD IN US...

Anaïs Nin

GRATEFUL FOR THE PEOPLE WHO MAKE LIFE RICH AND FULL.

NEVER FORGET... THAT ONE PERSON
CAN MAKE A DIFFERENCE...

R. Buckminster Fuller

GRATEFUL FOR THE
PEOPLE WHO CHANGE THINGS
FOR THE BETTER.

...WE BELONG TO EACH OTHER.

Mother Teresa

GRATEFUL FOR
THE PEOPLE WHOSE
LIVES ARE LINKED
WITH OURS.

...MY PREDOMINANT FEELING IS ONE OF GRATITUDE. I HAVE LOVED AND BEEN LOVED; I HAVE BEEN GIVEN MUCH AND I HAVE GIVEN SOMETHING IN RETURN...

Oliver Sacks

WHOSE PRESENCE IN
YOUR LIFE IS ONE YOU
GIVE THANKS FOR?

...FOR A *beautiful world*

AND EVERYTHING IN IT.

LOOK AT THE SKY: THAT IS FOR YOU.
LOOK AT EACH PERSON'S FACE AS YOU PASS
ON THE STREET: THOSE FACES ARE FOR YOU.

Miranda July

GRATEFUL FOR
THE BEAUTY THAT
FINDS US.

REMEMBER THAT EVERY
DAY CONTAINS A UNIVERSE
OF POTENTIAL...

Dominic Owen Mallary

GRATEFUL FOR
EACH MORNING
AND EVERY NEW
POSSIBILITY.

...EVERY GIFT IS EXACTLY THAT, A GIFT.

Maya Angelou

GRATEFUL FOR
ALL THAT THIS
DAY OFFERS.

...FIND ECSTASY IN LIVING...

Emily Dickinson

WHAT THINGS IN YOUR LIFE RIGHT NOW ARE EVEN BETTER THAN YOU COULD HAVE IMAGINED?

...FOR EVERYTHING

THAT'S *here.*

LOOK AROUND. LOOK AT WHAT WE HAVE.

Bob Ross

GRATEFUL FOR THIS ASTONISHING WORLD.

GRATITUDE… TURNS WHAT WE HAVE
INTO ENOUGH, AND MORE.

Melody Beattie

GRATEFUL FOR ALL
THE GOOD THINGS THAT
ARE ALREADY OURS.

THIS IS IT. NORMAL, DAILY LIFE...
IS THE MOST PRECIOUS THING...

Shauna Niequist

GRATEFUL JUST
FOR BEING.

...KEEP SAYING THANK YOU,
FOREVER AND SINCERELY.

Elizabeth Gilbert

HOW WILL YOU EXPRESS YOUR GRATITUDE?

GRATEFUL FOR ALL

THAT IS TO COME.

COMPENDIUM®
live inspired

WITH SPECIAL THANKS TO THE ENTIRE COMPENDIUM FAMILY.

CREDITS:

WRITTEN & COMPILED BY: M.H. CLARK
DESIGNED BY: JESSICA PHOENIX
EDITED BY: KRISTIN EADE

LIBRARY OF CONGRESS CONTROL NUMBER: 2019935001
ISBN: 978-1-946873-80-4

1ST PRINTING. PRINTED IN CHINA WITH SOY AND METALLIC INKS.